What's for Breakfast?

N.K Forbes

What's For Breakfast?

Copyright © N.K. Forbes
Illustration copyright © N.K. Forbes

First Edition 2018
Published by Aly's Books

www.alysbooks.com
Your Book | Our Mission

Designed by Fish Biscuit

All rights reserved. No part of this book may be reproduced or transmitted in any form or by any means, electronic, mechanical, photocopying or otherwise without the prior permission of the publisher.

ISBN: 978-0-6480017-8-2

For Mr Jordi Pants

We should eat a **healthy Breakfast** every day, to ensure we have the energy to run, think and play!

What will you choose for breakfast today?

... a bowl of thick, gluggy
cockroach custard?

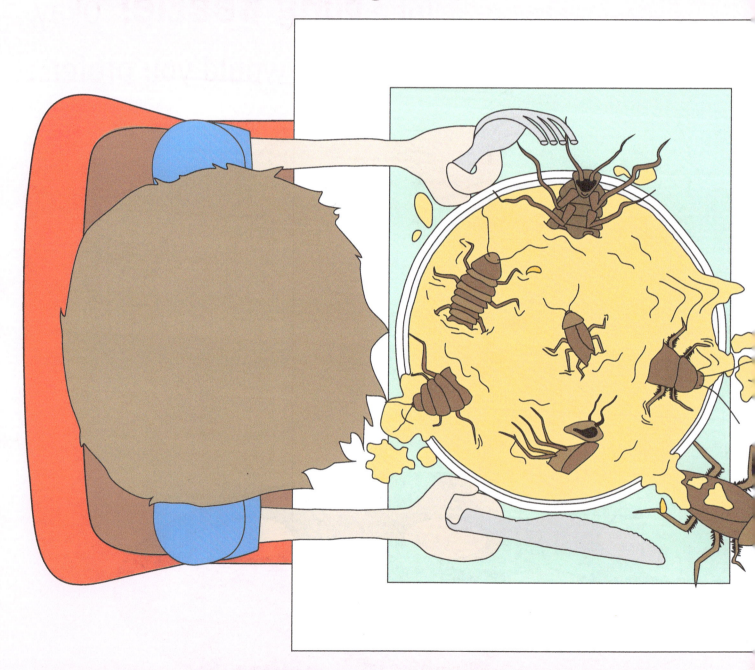

Oh? You don't like custard? Never mind, **roaches** taste better fried anyway.

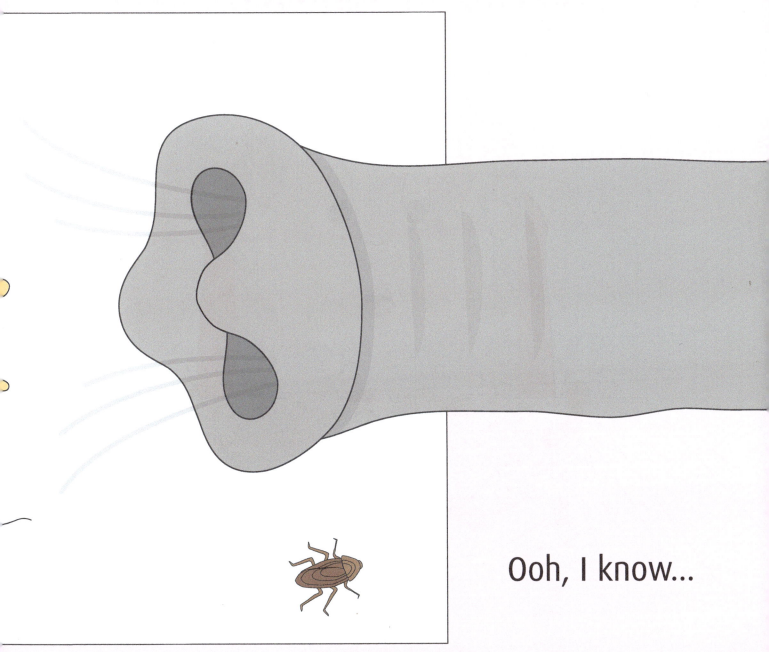

Ooh, I know...

A satisfying meal of wriggly, squirmy, **wormy spaghetti?**

Oh no, what a **noodle!**
Worms belong in the ground!

Let's see then,
what else have we got?

How about a soft, fluffy, SQUID SANDWICH?

You know, I had an **inkling** you would say no...
FYI squid is a delicacy in some cultures.

All right, should we make...

No, that **stinks.** Give that to Dad!

Perhaps you have a sweet tooth? Do you want...

What! Not the kind of **sprinkles** you were expecting? Well you had better choose soon I'm running out of ideas.

Will you try...

Eek! Me neither! It probably has a nasty **Bite.** NEXT!

Oh no! It looks like he's about to add his own topping! We should give him some **Privacy!**

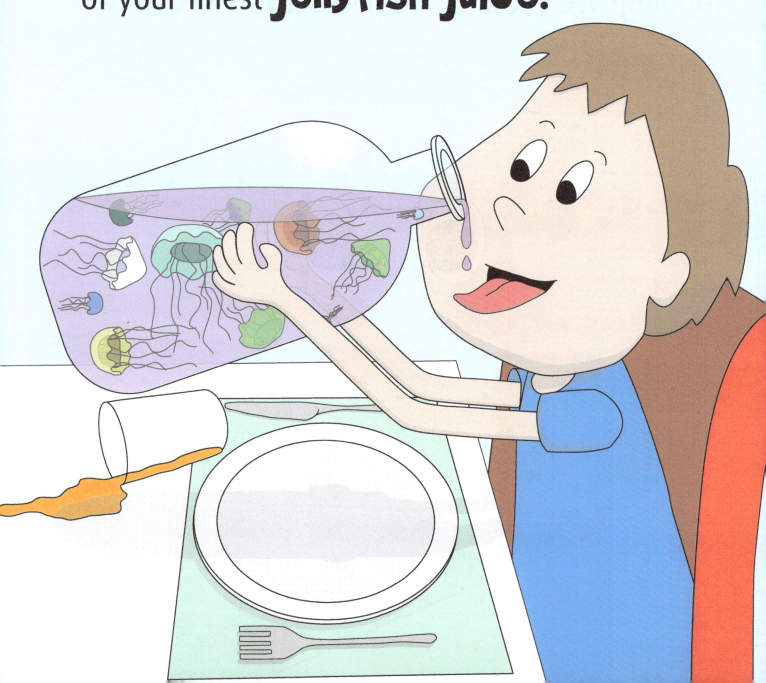

No? That doesn't **tantalize your tentacles?** Look, you're starting to get picky. Breakfast is the most important meal of the day, you know!

Perhaps you would like a **Bite-sized** breakfast instead?

Oh YUM! Crunchy little **Crocodile Crackers!**

Seriously? You don't want to **snap** these up? Okay, okay... let's mix it up with something a little less fancy.

Maybe you want a bubbling bowl of **Plain Porridge?**

PORRIDGE?

Are you **kidding** me? Of all the choices...

Why did I leave this decision up to you?

Oh well, I guess there's always tomorrow...

I am forever grateful, for your belief in me. You have helped my dream, become reality.

Shadi Almosri
Matt Babbington
Blake Barber
Maeve Bellmore
Belinda Britton
Riana Brockett
Emma Cotterill
Jennifer Dougas
Amanda Dyduk
Jordi Dyduk
Kendall Fitzwater
Alison Forbes
Helen Forbes
Keith Forbes
Lisa Forbes
Emily Fordham
Suzanne Fordham

Annick Foukal
Melissa Fyfe
Sally Hastings
Jesse Howard
Gregory Law
Tiffany Maynard
Valley Mein
Bugs Nash
Fadhila Prabu
Kylie Reeves
Margy Scott
Jakub Snabl
Coral Terlikowski
Susan Trigger
Clare Williamson
Chloe Wright